# BELOVED CHRISTMAS CLASSICS
# for
# BEGINNER VIOLINISTS

## Holiday Edition

### Easy violin solos with piano accompaniment

# INTRODUCTION

Beloved Classics for Solo Violinists is a multi-volume series of music books designed for mature beginners. The pieces within this collection have been long recognized as some of the most cherished works of all time. These classics have been adapted to allow musicians who are just starting their musical journey to enjoy creating beautiful music.

All of the pieces have been compiled and arranged by Kate & Kay Conservatory of Music. Digital downloads of the piano accompaniments can be downloaded by visiting:

**KateandKayLearningAcademy.com**

The digital downloads give the violinist the opportunity to practice with piano accompaniments.

# CONTENTS

4

Finger Position For A Major

# Away In A Manger

**Traditional Hymn**
**Arr: Kate & Kay Convservatory of Music**

# Silent Night

F. Gruber
Arr: Kate & Kay Conservatory of Music

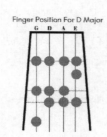

Finger Position For G Major

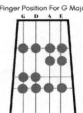

# Oh, Come, All Ye Faithful

J.F. Wade
Arr: Kate & Kay Conservatory of Music

# The First Noel

Traditional English Carol
Arr: Kate and Kay Conservatory of Music

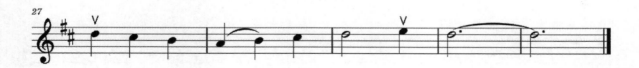

8

Finger Position For G Major

# We Three Kings of Orient Are

J.H. Hopkins
Arr: Kate & Kay Conservatory of Music

7

13

20

27

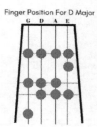

Finger Position For D Major

# Joy To The World

G.F. Handel
Arr: Kate & Kay Conservatory of Music

10

# O Holy Night

A.C. Adam
Arr: Kate & Kay Conservatory of Music

# Go Tell It On The Mountain

Traditional
Arr: Kate & Kay Conservatory of Music

12

# In The Bleak Midwinter

G. Holst
**Arr: Kate & Kay Conservatory of Music**

# Jesu, Joy of Man's Desiring

13

J.S. Bach

14

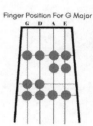

# O Come, O Come Emanuel

Traditional
Arr: Kate & Kay Conservatory of Music

# Ava Maria

F. Schubert
Arr: Kate & Kay Conservatory of Music

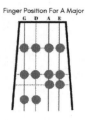

# Piano Accompaniments

# Away In A Manger

Traditional Hymn
Arr: Kate & Kay Convservatory of Music

# Silent Night

F. Gruber
Arr: Kate & Kay Conservatory of Music

# Oh, Come, All Ye Faithful

J.F. Wade
Arr: Kate & Kay Conservatory of Music

# The First Noel

Traditional English Carol
Arr: Kate and Kay Conservatory of Music

# We Three Kings of Orient Are

J.H. Hopkins
Arr: Kate & Kay Conservatory of Music

# Joy To The World

G.F. Handel
Arr: Kate & Kay Conservatory of Music

# O Holy Night

A.C. Adam
Arr: Kate & Kay Conservatory of Music

This page is intentionally left blank
to minimize page turns

# Go Tell It On The Mountain

Traditional
Arr: Kate & Kay Conservatory of Music

# In The Bleak Midwinter

G. Holst
Arr: Kate & Kay Conservatory of Music

# Jesu, Joy of Man's Desiring

J.S. Bach
Arranged by: Kate & Kay Conservatory of Music

# O Come, O Come Emanuel

Traditional
Arr: Kate & Kay Conservatory Of Music

# Ava Maria

F. Schubert
Arr: Kate & Kay Conservatory of Music

40

Made in the USA
Las Vegas, NV
20 November 2024

12188079R00024